A VISIT TO China

REVISED AND UPDATED

NORTH AMERICA

ASIA

CHINA

AUSTRALIA

Peter and Connie Roop

Heinemann
LIBRARY

www.heinemann.co.uk/library
Visit our website to find out more information about Heinemann Library books.

To order:
 Phone 44 (0) 1865 888066
 Send a fax to 44 (0) 1865 314091
Visit the Heinemann Bookshop at www.heinemann.co.uk/library to browse our catalogue and order online.

First published in Great Britain by Heinemann Library, Halley Court, Jordan Hill, Oxford OX2 8EJ, part of Pearson Education. Heinemann is a registered trademark of Pearson Education Ltd.

© Pearson Education Ltd 1998, 2008

Editorial: Diyan Leake
Design: Joanna Hinton-Malivoire and Philippa Jenkins
Picture research: Mica Brancic
Production: Duncan Gilbert

Originated by Chroma Graphics (Overseas) Pte Ltd
Printed in Hong Kong.

ISBN 978 0 431 087344 (hardback)
12 11 10 09 08
10 9 8 7 6 5 4 3 2 1

ISBN 978 0 431 087481 (paperback)
12 11 10 09 08
10 9 8 7 6 5 4 3 2 1

British Library Cataloguing in Publication Data
Roop, Peter
 A visit to China
 1. China – Social conditions – 2000 –   – Juvenile literature
 2. China – Geography – Juvenile literature
 3. China – Social life and customs – 2002 –   – Juvenile literature
 I.Title II. Roop, Connie III. China
 951'.06

Acknowledgements
The publishers would like to thank the following for permission to reproduce photographs: © Alamy p. **25** (Tom Salyer/Punchstock); © Biofotos p. **27** (G&P Corrigan); © Corbis p. **22** (Michael Prince); © Getty Images p. **20** (China Photos); © Heather Angel pp. **16**, **18**, **19**, **24**; © Hutchison Library pp. **8** (T. Page), **11** (S. Errington), **13**, **17** (F. Greene), **26** (T. Page); © J. Allan Cash Ltd p. **6**; © Photolibrary p. **5** (Robert Harding Travel/ Angelo Cavalli); © Reuters pp. **10** (Nir Elias), **21** (Simon Zo); © Trip pp. **7** (J. Batten), **9** (A. Tovy), **12** (K. Cardwell), **14** (F. Good), **15** (B. Vikander), **23** (F. Good), **28** (F. Good); © Zefa p. **29**.

Cover photograph reproduced with permission of © Getty Images (Glow Images).

Our thanks to Nick Lapthorn for his comments in the preparation of this book.

Every effort has been made to contact copyright holders of any material reproduced in this book. Any omissions will be rectified in subsequent printings if notice is given to the publishers.

Contents

Any words appearing in bold, **like this**, are explained in the Glossary.

China

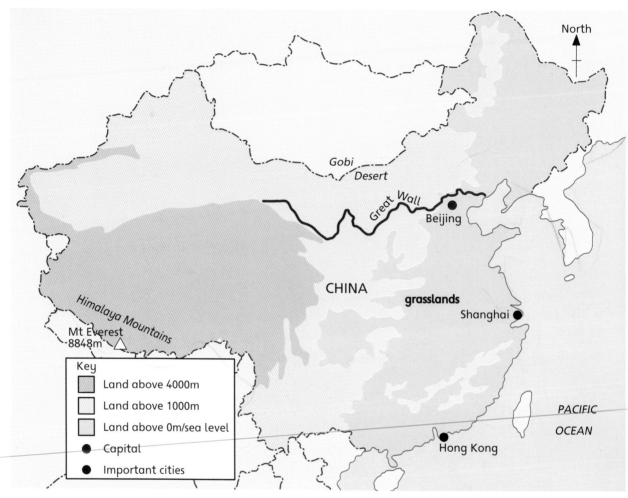

North

Gobi Desert

Great Wall

Beijing

CHINA

grasslands

Shanghai

Himalaya Mountains

Mt Everest 8848m

Key
- Land above 4000m
- Land above 1000m
- Land above 0m/sea level
- Capital
- Important cities

Hong Kong

PACIFIC OCEAN

More people live in China than in any other country. The Chinese make up one-fifth of all the people in the world.

China is in Asia. It is one of the largest countries in the world. The Chinese call their home the Middle Kingdom.

This is a street in Shanghai, the city in China with the most people.

China **slopes** down from the Himalaya Mountains to the Pacific Ocean. Mount Everest, the highest mountain on Earth, is in the Himalaya Mountains.

The middle of China is covered with **grasslands** and **deserts**. Most people live in the east, where the green lowlands slope down to the sea.

The Gobi Desert in is the middle of China.

Landmarks

The Great Wall of China stretches for 6314 kilometres (3923 miles). It would take you a week to drive from one end to the other! The Wall was built long ago to keep out China's enemies.

Thousands of people visit the Forbidden City every day.

The **capital** city of China is Beijing. Many people go to Beijing to see the Forbidden City. It used to be the palace for the **emperor**.

Homes

Most city homes and flats are small. They have two or three rooms. Families share bathrooms and kitchens with neighbours.

Most Chinese people live in the countryside. Often grandparents, parents, and children share the same house.

Homes in the countryside are larger than homes in the cities.

Food

Most meals are rice or noodles, with small pieces of meat or vegetables. A favourite Chinese food is **dumplings**. People eat with **chopsticks** or spoons.

China also has tea houses. There you can drink tea and eat lots of sweet, sticky cakes. Chinese people do not put milk in their tea.

Clothes

In the country, people wear loose, baggy clothes. They need to be comfortable while they work in the fields. In the cities, most Chinese people wear modern clothes.

On special occasions, many Chinese
people dress up. They wear the
colourful clothes of their **region**.

Work

Most Chinese people are farmers. They grow rice, tea, wheat, or vegetables. Some farmers also keep chickens, pigs, ducks, or fish.

Products made in Chinese factories are sold all around the world.

Chinese workers make iron, steel, chemicals, oil, and machines. China sells many of these **products** and others, like toys or food, to other countries.

Transport

Most Chinese people travel by foot, bicycle, boat, or bus. More and more people get around by car.

Big ships from around the world visit China's busy **ports**.

Trains and lorries carry people and **products** across China. Chinese boats, called junks, sail on rivers and canals.

Languages

Most people in China are called Han Chinese. They speak Mandarin Chinese.

These people are Hu Chinese.

There are also 55 other groups of people in China. These people live, dress, and speak differently from the Han Chinese.

School

Children from the age of 6 to 12 go to elementary school. They learn science, maths, Chinese, English, history, geography, art, and physical education.

Each Chinese character has its own meaning.

Chinese children must learn to read around 3500 **characters**. Adults who read many books can read around 6000 characters.

Free time

Chinese children spend a lot of time helping at home. In their free time, they play football, basketball, volleyball, table tennis, and chess. They also like making and flying kites.

Most Chinese people exercise every day. They ride bicycles to work or do kung fu. People also dance or do a stretching exercise called t'ai chi.

Groups of people often do t'ai chi together.

Celebrations

Everyone tries to be at home for the Spring Festival. People dress up in their best clothes, visit friends, and eat cakes. They also enjoy lion dancing in the **parades.**

People in uniform take part in parades to celebrate National Day.

National Day celebrates the **founding** of the People's Republic of China. People celebrate with sports, bands, parades, and noisy fireworks.

The Arts

China is famous for its pictures of nature on **china**, paper, and silk. Other popular Chinese arts are cutting delicate pictures out of paper and painting **characters** with a paintbrush.

The costume shows how important an opera character is.

Chinese people enjoy the **opera**. The clever, kind Monkey King is a favourite opera **character**. The **audience** shout, "Hao!" when they like an actor's performance.

Factfile

Name	The full name of China is the People's Republic of China.
Capital	The **capital** city is Beijing.
Language	Most Chinese people speak Mandarin Chinese.
Population	There are more than 1.3 billion people living in China.
Money	Chinese money is called the yuan.
Religions	Many Chinese people believe in Taoism, Confucianism, Buddhism, Islam, or Christianity.
Products	China produces lots of coal, rice, machines, oil, steel and cement.

Words you can learn

ni hao (nee how)	hello
zaijian (zay-GEE-en)	goodbye
xiexie (SHE-a-shay)	thank you
shide (SURE-duh)	yes
bu shi (BOO sure)	no
yi	one
er	two
san	three

Glossary

audience group of people who watch something

capital city where the government is based

character mark used in the Chinese writing system. A character is also a person in a story.

china a material made from fine clay used for making plates and cups

chopsticks a pair of sticks held in one hand to lift food to the mouth

course stage in a meal, like pudding

desert large area of land that has almost no rain and very few plants and animals

dumplings dough mixture with meats and vegetables inside, which is cooked in boiling water or steam

emperor person like a king, who ruled China a long time ago

founding beginning

grasslands large, flat areas of land where grasses are the only plants that grow

opera a play with music and singing

parade group of people on show, dancing or walking together

port place where ships pick up and drop off the goods they are carrying

products things which are grown, taken from the earth, made by hand, or made in a factory

region area or part of a country

slope to go from high up to lower down

Index